I0817210

For Presley, her brother Asher, and curious children everywhere who love the natural world.

– Susan Lamb

To the Lewis family, Jacquie and Otto.

– Sean Lewis

This is a first edition published in 2024
by Flying Eye Books Ltd. 27 Westgate Street, London E8 3RL.

With special thanks to Lance Polingyouma

Edited by Sara Forster
Designed by Riko Sekiguchi

1 2 3 4 5 6 7 8 9 10

Published in the US by Flying Eye Books Ltd.
Printed in China on FSC® certified paper.

ISBN: 978-1-83874-160-0

www.flyingeyebooks.com

SUSAN LAMB

SEAN LEWIS

EARTH'S INCREDIBLE PLACES
GRAND CANYON

FLYING EYE BOOKS

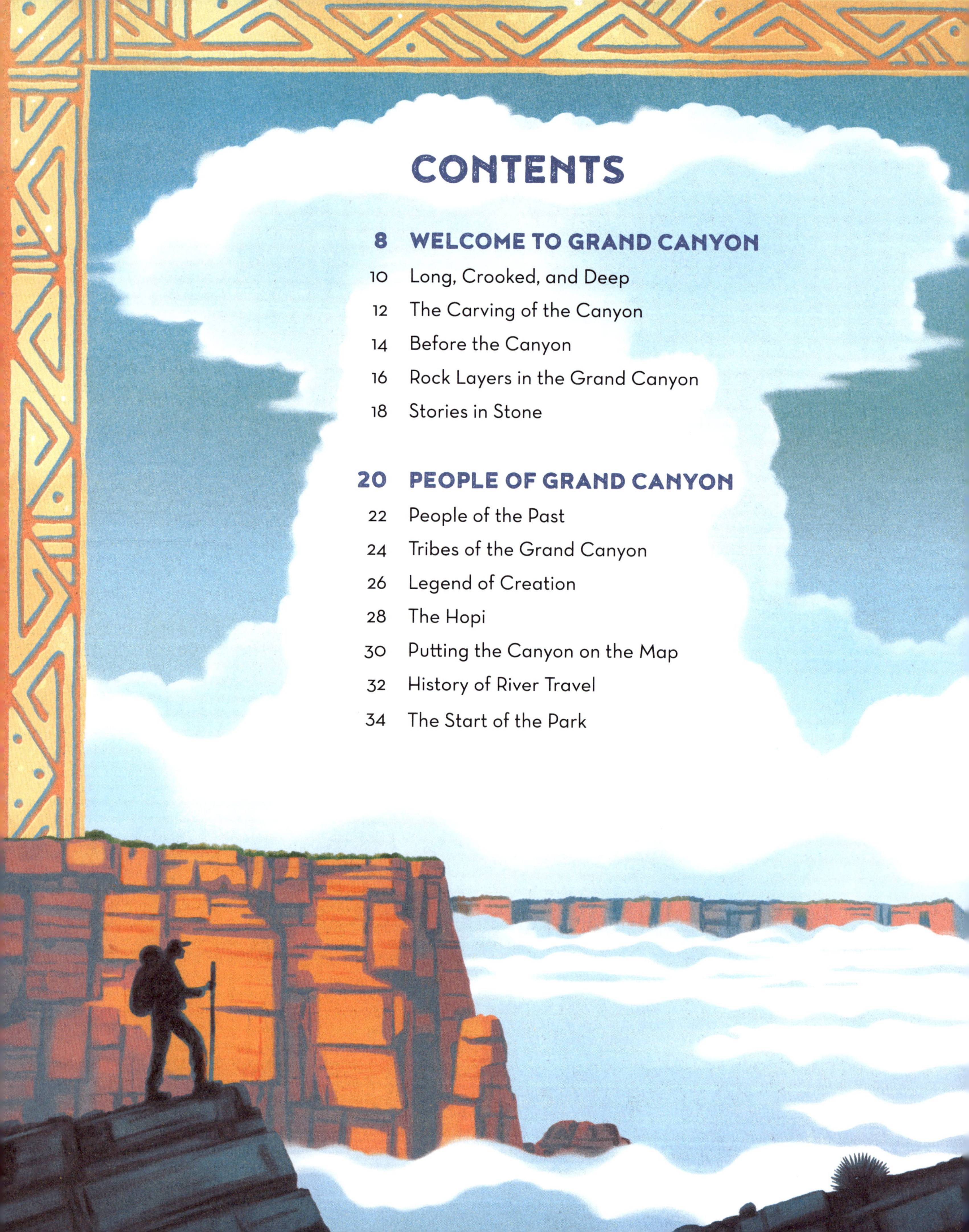

CONTENTS

INTRODUCTION

Stretching across a rocky **plateau** in America, carved deep into the rocks by the rushing Colorado River, lies the Grand Canyon. Its bands of rock tells us about millions of years of our planet's history and the amazing variety of plants and animals from the past to the present. Today, hawks soar high on warm air from deep in the canyon. Bighorn sheep leap up and down the cliffs. Mountain lions prowl the forests.

The Grand Canyon has captured humankind's imagination since the Ice Age. Now it is your turn to explore!

WELCOME TO
GRAND CANYON

LONG, CROOKED, AND DEEP

A canyon is a deep, narrow valley with steep sides. The Grand Canyon is cut into the high Colorado Plateau of the American Southwest. It is 6,000 feet deep and as much as 18 miles wide. Grand Canyon National Park covers 1,902 square miles as it twists for 277 miles along the Colorado River.

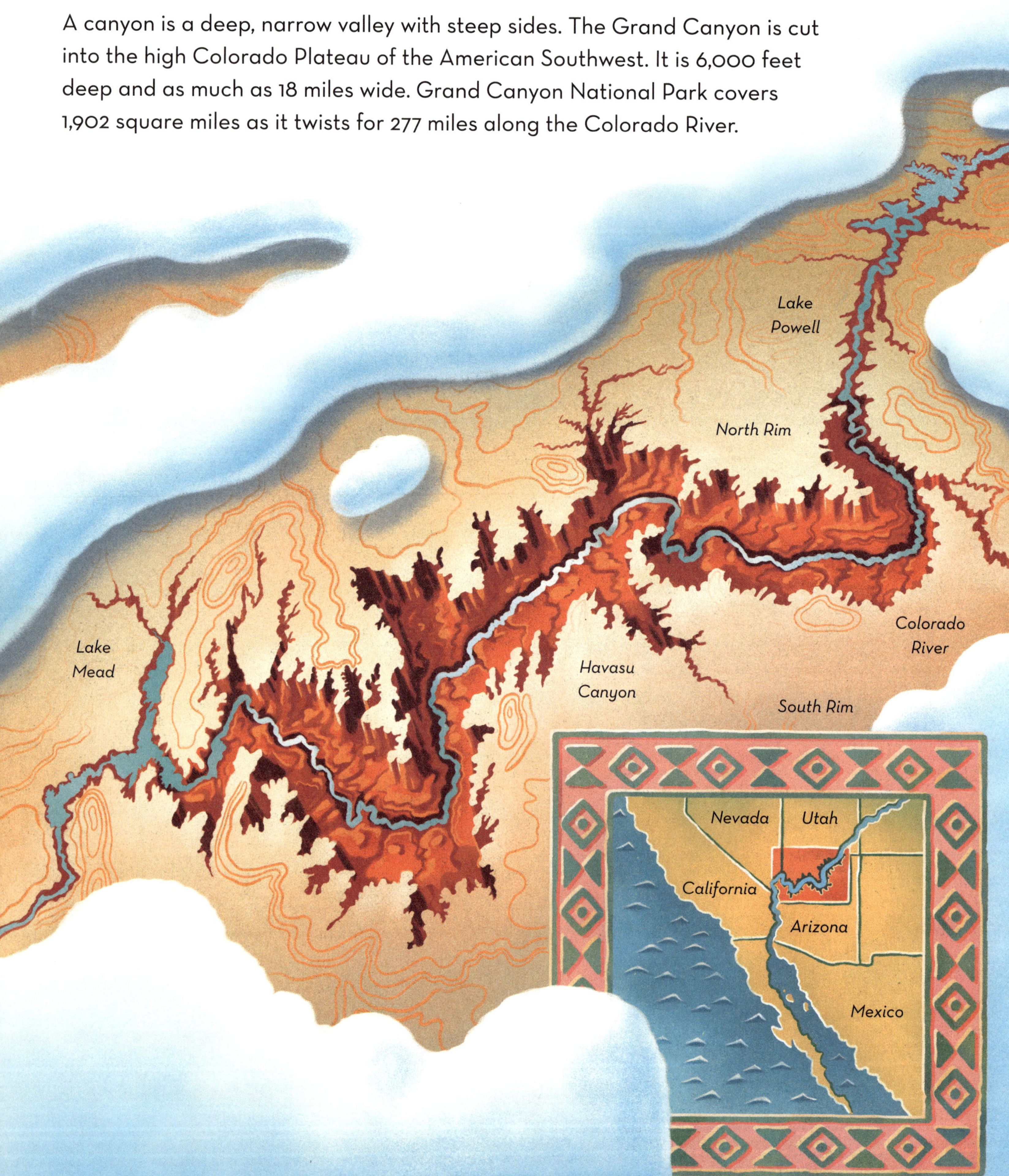

A LONG DESERT RIVER

The Colorado River begins in the Rocky Mountains. It flows 1,450 miles to the Sea of Cortez in Mexico. The river provides water to lots of farms and to about 40 million people in the US and Mexico. Many dams along its length use the river's power to make electricity. They create lakes where people swim, fish, and waterski. After years of dry weather, the river is very low now.

HIGH, WIDE, AND LONESOME

People have lived on the Colorado Plateau for at least 13,000 years. It is a rocky place with a dry climate. The plateau averages 6,352 feet above sea level and covers 150,580 square miles. People come from all over the world to see its colorful cliffs and canyons.

EXPLORING THE PARK

Five million people visit the Grand Canyon every year. They travel by car, or by train on the historic Grand Canyon Railway. They explore the canyon's rim on foot, by bicycle, or bus. Some hike into the canyon, while others ride mules. A few camp overnight. Some lucky people float down the Colorado River in rafts or boats.

THE CARVING OF THE CANYON

When you stand on the rim of the Grand Canyon, you can hear the Colorado River roaring 6,000 feet below you. The river began to carve the canyon less than six million years ago.

SHAPING THE CANYON

The Colorado River is powerful because it is steep. The river can carry more than 500,000 tons of sediment through the canyon in a day. The sediment helps grind the canyon deeper and deeper.

1.

Over time, the river ground down a channel through different kinds and colors of rock.

2.

Softer rocks crumbled into slopes that left space under the harder rocks above them. Then the harder rocks broke off and formed cliffs.

3.

Swift-flowing creeks cut side canyons into the rim and made the canyon wider. They left ridges, mountains, and plateaus between the side canyons.

CREATING A CANYON

Flowing water is the most powerful cause of erosion, but it doesn't work alone.

On cold nights, water freezes and expands in cracks in the canyon walls, which widens them.

Plant roots pry apart rocks and gravity tugs rocks down the canyon walls.

Large rocks roll down creeks and form big, noisy rapids in the river.

Rain mixes with carbon dioxide in the air to form a weak acid that dissolves rock.

BEFORE THE CANYON

The Grand Canyon cuts through many layers of very old rocks. Long ago, the rocks began as deserts, rivers, and ocean floors. **Geologists** sort them into three kinds of rocks that formed in three different ways.

SEDIMENTARY ROCK

These rocks form when water and wind carry tiny particles of things like sand, mud, and even living things like plants, shells, or bones from one place to settle in another. Over time, more particles settle on top, squashing down the particles below to form rock.

IGNEOUS ROCK

When hot, melted rock cools it forms igneous rock. This can happen when melted rock escapes as lava through volcanoes and cools quickly on the surface, or while magma cools slowly under the ground. The speed at which the magma cools causes different types of rocks to form.

Under high heat and pressure, sandstone becomes quartzite.

METAMORPHIC ROCK

Very high heat and pressure squeeze sedimentary and igneous rocks into **metamorphic** rocks.

Granite is an igneous rock with bits of minerals that cooled slowly enough to grow into crystals.

WHY IS THERE SO MUCH HEAT AND PRESSURE?

The **mantle** is a layer of extremely hot rock around Earth's super-hot core.

The mantle rises up in currents, like boiling water. It cools near Earth's surface and sinks down again.

The magma pushes and pulls on Earth's crust, which is broken into **tectonic plates**.

The plates can crack or wrinkle causing faults when they run into each other, or push one another up or down.

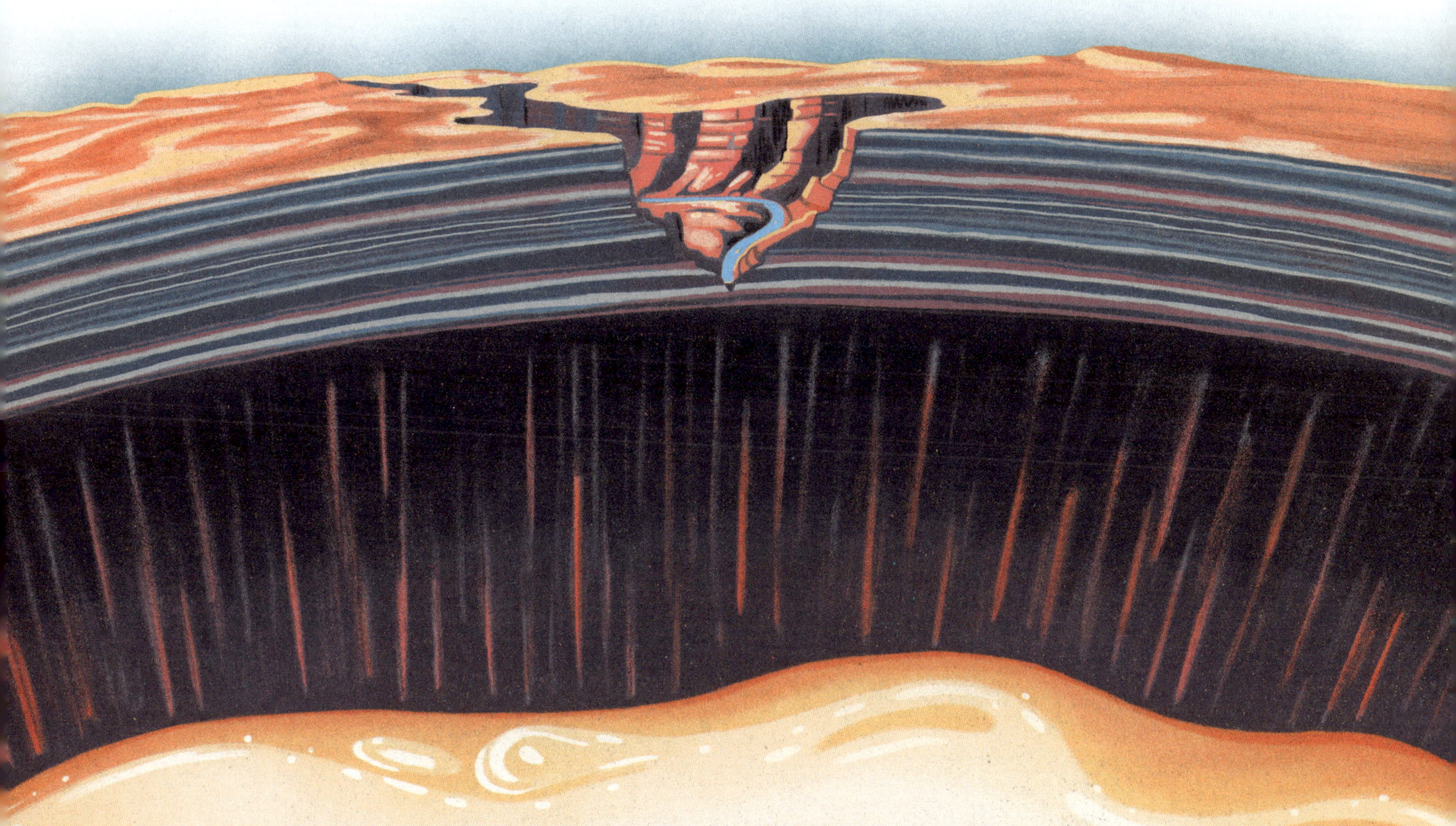

One plate can push another one up or down or wrinkle it into valleys and mountains. The Grand Canyon's top layer, the Kaibab Formation, began as the floor of an ancient sea but is now 7,000 feet above sea level.

ROCK LAYERS IN THE GRAND CANYON

There are more than forty layers of rock forming the walls of the Grand Canyon. The deeper you go, the older the rocks are. At the very bottom of the canyon the rocks are almost 1.75 billion years old.

1. KAIBAB FORMATION

This layer is mostly limestone. It is 270 million years old and contains lots of fossils of sea creatures. Later, more rock layers formed on top of the Kaibab. They have eroded away but can be seen at other southwestern national parks, including Zion and Bryce Canyon.

2. COCONINO SANDSTONE

The swirling coconino sandstone has been called the canyon's "bathtub ring." It began as sand dunes in a vast desert like the Sahara. Wind blew the sand in different directions. We can still see layers of sand crossing over each other.

3. BRIGHT ANGEL SHALE

This layer is a purple and green slope on top of a steep cliff. It is full of marine **fossils** such as **trilobites**. Its unusual green color is from glauconite, a mineral that forms in shallow seas with lots of decaying animal life but not much oxygen.

4. GRAND CANYON SUPERGROUP

This group began on the bottom of a shallow sea. Mud settled there along with layers full of tiny forms of early life, sand, and other minerals. Waves and tides made ripples in the layers. After they became rock, plates of Earth's crust moved and tilted the layers up into mountains. Erosion wore down most of these mountains.

5. VISHNU BASEMENT ROCKS

The layer at the bottom of the canyon began as thick silt on a sea floor. Volcanoes spread patches of lava there too. Then plates of Earth's crust moved, squeezing the silt and lava into high mountains of dark rocks known as schists. Melted rock oozed up into the mountains and cooled into pink-and-white Zoroaster Granite.

STORIES IN STONE

The Grand Canyon's sedimentary rocks contain fossils. Fossils preserve animals, plants, and the markings they made that were trapped between layers of sediment. All canyon layers above the supergroup belong to the **Paleozoic era**, the "time of ancient life" long before dinosaurs walked the Earth.

TRACKS AND SEEDS

Rock layers formed in sand, swamps, and lakes. On sand dunes, egg-laying animals with four feet, like lizards, made the oldest **vertebrate** tracks found in the canyon so far.

Reptiles and **amphibians** made footprints in the damp dunes of the Coconino Sandstone. Spiders, scorpions, beetles, and millipedes left tracks there too.

Clubmosses, **seed ferns**, horsetails, pines, and gingko trees left impressions in the mud. The atmosphere held more oxygen then and insects were larger. A dragonfly left a print of its 8-inch long wing.

UNDER THE SEA

Three hundred and twenty million years ago, sea creatures with cartilage instead of bone appeared such as sharks, rays, and rat fish. Their teeth and spines remain as fossils.

Brachiopods

Crinoids

Trilobites

Marine animals with hinged shells like clams are called **brachiopods**. They are the most common fossils in the rocks of Grand Canyon.

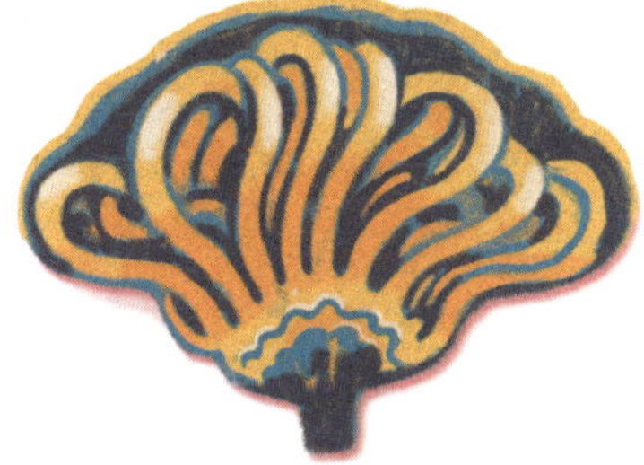

Relatives of starfish and sea urchins are **crinoids**. Feathery arms around their mouths collect tiny plants and animals called **plankton**.

Trilobites have bodies with three sections covered in plates. Some species have complex eyes with 15,000 lenses.

PEOPLE OF GRAND CANYON

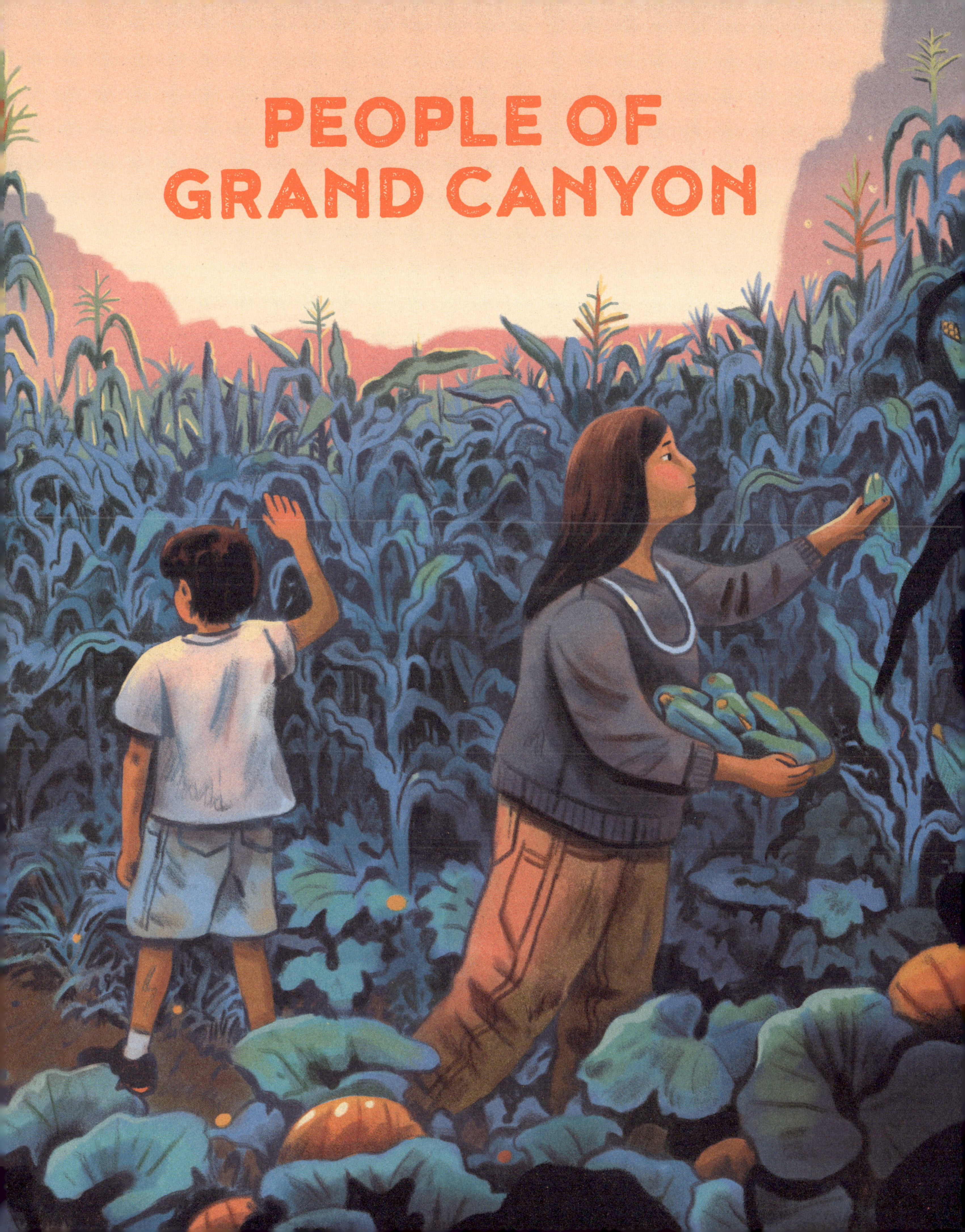

PEOPLE OF THE PAST

People have lived at the Grand Canyon for thousands of years. **Archaeologists** have found **artifacts** that tell us about how people used to live. As well as baskets, pottery, spears, and dwellings, there are images created on stone. These tell of the **ceremonies** people held, the stories they told, and the music they made. Such finds are very important to the tribes whose **ancestors** once lived here.

At least 12,000 to 10,000 years ago	Around 10,000 to 3,000 years ago	Around 3,000 years ago to 750 CE

PALEO-AMERICAN

Near the end of the last Ice Age, a Clovis hunter left a broken spear point in the canyon. The Clovis people made many tools from stone and bone and hunted **megafauna**—large mammals, such as Shasta ground sloths.

ARCHAIC

Archaic people lived in family groups. They moved from place to place, hunting and gathering according to the season. They also bent twigs into animal shapes and painted or chipped pictures on the canyon walls.

BASKETMAKER

At first, Basketmakers were hunter-gatherers who lived in simple shelters. Around 500 CE, they began farming, and settled down in **pithouses**. They made pottery, hunted with bows and arrows, and wove blankets, sandals, bags, and baskets.

Around 750 CE to 1300

ANCESTRAL PUEBLOAN

Ancestral Puebloans hunted, gathered, and farmed crops such as corn and cotton. Much of their pottery was beautifully painted. They lived in small **pueblos** and built stone cities across the region.

Around 600 CE to 1150

COHONINA

Cohonina is the Hopi name for Supai people who lived at the western end of the Grand Canyon and farmed near the mouth of Havasu Canyon. The Cohonina coated their plain pottery with ocher, a natural red dye that they traded with other tribes.

Around 1300 to 1540

PROTOHISTORIC PERIOD

Ancestors of today's Southern Paiute and Navajo people moved with the seasons, living in simple rock, driftwood, or brush shelters.

TRIBES OF THE GRAND CANYON

Today, there are many **Native** American tribes who remember their Grand Canyon ancestors and tell stories about the canyon in their own languages.

ZUÑI

Zuñi spoken history says they come from Ribbon Falls in the Grand Canyon. Today they live along the Zuñi River in New Mexico, and are famous for their carvings of tiny animals.

SOUTHERN PAIUTE

Southern Paiutes hunted and gathered in a vast area north of the Grand Canyon. Today, they make beautiful baskets for their own use and for sale.

NAVAJO

The Navajo probably arrived in the Southwest around 1300. They learned how to farm and weave from Puebloan people, and began raising livestock after Spanish settlers brought sheep, cattle, and horses to the area.

YAVAPAI-APACHE

These two tribes have their own languages and cultures. They hunted, gathered, and farmed near each other, and now share a **reservation**.

HAVASUPAI & HUALAPAI

The Havasupai and Hualapai still live within the Grand Canyon today. Havasupai means "people of the blue-green waters" and Hualapai means "people of the tall trees."

The Hualapai live south of the Colorado River. Their land covers 108 miles of the canyon rim, and grasslands and mountains to the south where they raise cattle and harvest trees to make timber.

The Havasupai farm in Havasu Canyon, deep in the Grand Canyon. Most live in Supai, a village 8 miles from the nearest road that is famous for nearby blue-green waterfalls.

LEGEND OF CREATION

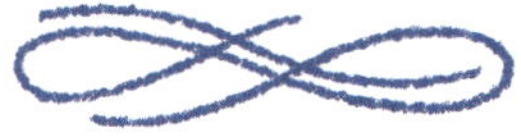

Tochopo and Hokomata were brothers at the beginning of time. Tochopo was good and kind but Hokomata was the opposite, always causing trouble. One day, Hokomata grew angry with Tochopo and swore to drown the whole world. To save his daughter, Pukeheh, Tochopo hollowed out the trunk of a pinyon tree and made a window in it. He sadly said goodbye to his little girl, sealed her inside the tree with some food, and waited.

Rain poured down, as if from countless waterfalls. The roar of the water was louder than a thousand Colorado Rivers. The pinyon log floated, keeping Pukeheh safe as the water reached higher than the mountains.

After some years, the rain finally stopped. The water rushed down to the sea, cutting the Grand Canyon deep into the earth. Pukeheh felt the log come to a rest and looked out of the window. It was very dark but she could see the Little Colorado River canyon to the north and the Grand Canyon to the west. She climbed out and began to make baskets and pottery, as she had learned years ago when she was a child.

The sun rose and light returned to the world. Pukeheh and the sun had a son named Inyaa. She carried the child west to Havasu Canyon, where she and one of the waterfalls had a baby girl together. The two children grew up to become the parents of all human beings. To this day, girls of the Havasupai tribe are called "daughters of the water."

THE HOPI

Hopi people (*Hopisenom*) have deep roots in the Grand Canyon, going back to the ancestral Puebloans (*Hisatsinom*) who lived there from 550 BCE until about 1300 CE.

YAI-NI-NII, THE BEGINNING

Hopi clans arrived at different times from different places. Each has its own knowledge, stories, and responsibilities to its village. Hopi tradition says humans climbed up from three earlier worlds, changing in form and behavior in each one. Two supernatural beings who came with them created mountains, plains, and *Öngtupqa*—the Grand Canyon.

A FARMING CULTURE

Farming is at the heart of Hopi society and religion. They believe that the Creator of the World gave their people corn to grow. The Hopi made an agreement with this Creator and were allowed to stay if they cared for the Earth. Farming is very difficult in their dry and windy homeland but Hopi succeed by staying true to their ancient teachings.

SIGNS OF THE PAST

Today, the Hopi live east of the Grand Canyon, close enough to walk there on pilgrimages. Signs of their ancestors— especially a type of rock carving called a petroglyph—can be seen across the vast landscape around them.

HOPI HOMES

Traditional Hopi homes resemble those of ancestral Puebloans. Their stone apartments cluster together in twelve villages called pueblos. These pueblos are built on the top of mesas, steep-sided, flat-topped hills. The people gather for stories, ceremonies, and talk of village concerns in **kivas**. Kivas are large round or square rooms, often underground, which are entered by a ladder through the roof. Kivas today still look like those used in the past.

PUTTING THE CANYON ON THE MAP

The Grand Canyon wasn't always a popular tourist site. When the first Europeans visited, they were only interested in using the canyon as a transport route, or as a place to mine minerals. It took a while for them to realize the canyon's potential for scientific research and as a tourist destination.

EARLY EXPLORERS

The first Europeans to see the Grand Canyon were Spanish soldiers under the command of García López de Cárdenas. They had been sent to scout a "great river" that could be used to reach the Gulf of California by boat. They arrived on the South Rim in September, 1540, but after four days of failing to reach the river, they turned back.

NAMING THE RIVER

In 1776, Father Francisco Tomás Garcés arrived on horseback in Hualapai country. The Hualapai received him kindly and took him to meet the Havasupai, who entertained Garcés for five days, then took him back to the rim where he could see the vast canyon. Garcés called the river *Colorado*, the Spanish word for "rusty-red."

STEAMBOAT EXPEDITION

In 1858, Lieutenant Joseph Christmas Ives of the US Army headed an **expedition** to see how far a steamboat could travel up the Colorado River. The boat hit rocks downriver of the Grand Canyon and most of the group turned back.

THE START OF TOURISM

In the 1880s, the first Europeans began settling around the rim of the Grand Canyon. They hoped to make their fortunes mining but soon realized that it was more profitable to rent horses and mules to tourists than to mine.

BUILDING DESIGN

In 1901, architect Mary Jane Colter began designing buildings at the Grand Canyon. Colter combined ideas from ancient pueblos, early Spanish buildings, and western ranches with local stone and Native American art. The buildings she designed, including the Desert View Watchtower and Lookout Studio, are still in use today.

THE PHOTOGRAPHERS

In 1903, brothers Emery and Ellsworth Kolb built a studio perched over the Bright Angel Trail to take pictures of tourists riding by on mules. They would then run more than 4 miles down the trail to develop the film, and run back up to be ready to sell the pictures to the tourists as they returned.

THE CIVILIAN CONSERVATION CORPS

The Civilian Conservation Corps (CCC) was a government program that aimed to employ young men during the Great Depression. In 1933, the CCC arrived at the Grand Canyon to fight forest fires and build roads, trails, stone walls, shelters, and picnic areas. Much of their work is still in use today.

HISTORY OF RIVER TRAVEL

Rafting the Colorado River through the Grand Canyon takes great strength and skill. At least eighty major rapids and countless boulders, waves, and eddies make it a challenge for even the most experienced river runners.

Running the river changed when Glen Canyon Dam was completed in 1964. River runners now adapt to constantly changing water levels that depend on how much hydroelectric power the dam must generate for distant cities.

THE HOPI

Centuries ago, a Hopi named Ma-um climbed into a hollowed-out log and floated down the river in search of rain. Along the way, he met people who knew a ceremony to bring rain. Ma-um married a woman and they brought her peoples' ceremony back to the cornfields.

THE GEOLOGIST

In 1869, geologist John Wesley Powell led the first river trip down the Colorado River through the Grand Canyon. For three dangerous and exhausting weeks, his men steered past rocks and ran rapids.

THE RIVER BOTANISTS

In 1938, **botanists** Elzada Clover and Lois Jotter were the first non-Native women to run the river through the canyon. Rowed by adventurer Norman Nevills, they made the first study and collection of canyon plants.

THE RIVER GUIDE

Kim Crumbo was a member of the Citizen Potawatomi Tribe. After returning from service as a Navy SEAL in Vietnam, he became famous for his courage and compassion as a river ranger at the canyon. Later, he worked tirelessly to preserve wild places for both wildlife and humanity.

THE RIVER RANGER

Havasupai Shana Watahomigie was the first Native American female river ranger. Shana introduced passengers and fellow river runners to the canyon's human story and natural wonders. In 2006, she rowed a crew down the river to make a film about water conservation.

THE START OF THE PARK

Grand Canyon became a national park because the public wanted to preserve it. Illustrated reports published by explorers showed people the canyon's wild magnificence compared to factories and crowded cities.

THIRD TIME LUCKY

Senator Benjamin Harrison tried to make it a national park three times. Later, as president, Harrison established the Grand Cañon Forest Preserve but mining, logging, and cattle grazing were still allowed.

THE EARLY YEARS

Famous naturalists John Muir and John Burroughs campaigned for more protection. President Teddy Roosevelt declared it "the one great sight every American should see." He made parts of it a federal game preserve and later, a national monument.

SETTING UP THE PARK

Congress established the National Park Service in 1916, to protect national parks and monuments and "leave them unimpaired for the enjoyment of future generations." They created Grand Canyon National Park three years later. The National Park Service gradually stopped logging, mining, and cattle grazing, and placed limits on new building.

EXPANDING THE PARK

A 1975 law expanded the park to include the western canyon and Marble Canyon to the north. It restored 185,000 acres on the canyon rim to the Havasupai and gave them exclusive use of another 95,000 acres from the rim to the river.

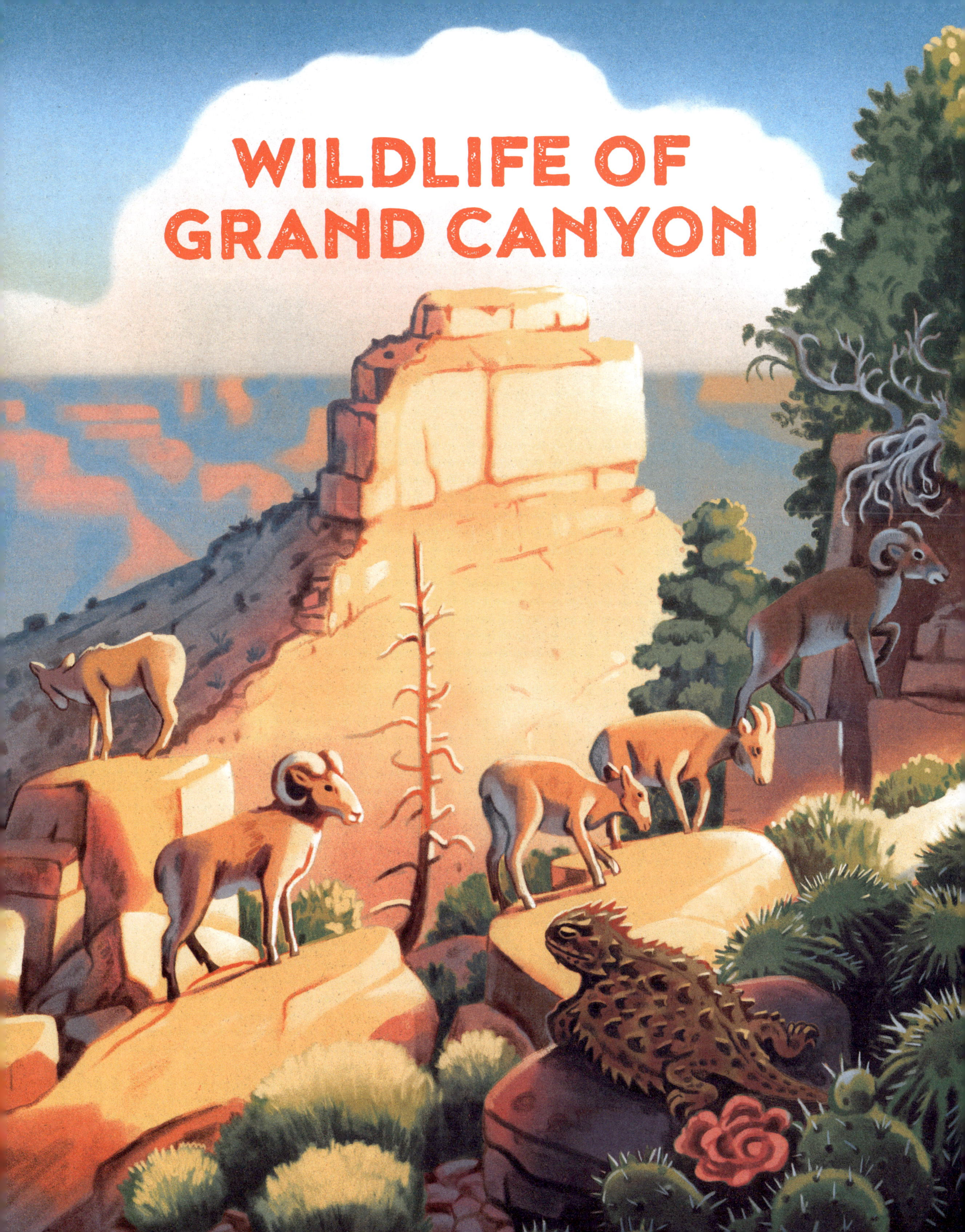
WILDLIFE OF
GRAND CANYON

THE GRAND CANYON ECOSYSTEM

An **ecosystem** is a complete community of living things, together with landscape, water, and climate where they live. At the Grand Canyon, the climate becomes warmer and drier the deeper you go. There is a desert at the bottom, but the water of the Colorado River makes it possible for many plants and animals to live there.

An area with its own climate, plants, and animals is called a life zone. There are five life zones from the top of the Grand Canyon to the bottom. Each of these life zones is home to a specific group of plants and animals, which make up the biodiversity of the canyon.

Coyotes, mule deer, and gray foxes can live in any life zone. Some animals move between zones according to the season.

BOREAL FOREST

Above 8,200 feet

The boreal forest is the highest area on the North Rim. It is the coldest zone and gets the most rain and snow. The trees here grow tall and close together. There are open meadows too. Plants and animals here can survive the colder temperatures.

PONDEROSA PINE FOREST

Above 7,000 to 8,200 feet

Ponderosa pine forests grow along both rims of the Grand Canyon. The growing season is longer than in the boreal forest and there are more plants and animals.

PINYON-JUNIPER WOODLAND

Above 4,500 to 7,500 feet

Pinyon pines and juniper trees grow on the upper canyon walls. Trees are shorter because the climate is drier. It is a good place for rodents and birds that eat the nuts and berries from the trees.

DESERT SCRUB

Above 1,500 to 4,500 feet

The desert scrub is a very dry, hot zone. Many animals visit in spring and leave when it becomes too warm during the hot, dry summers. Plants like cacti and agaves thrive, along with scorpions, snakes, and other reptiles.

RIPARIAN

The riparian ecosystem is found along the edges of creeks, springs, and rivers in the Grand Canyon basin. Plants and animals here, such as cottonwood trees, frogs, and toads, need lots of water to survive.

PONDEROSA PINE FORESTS

Stretching up to 200 feet tall, ponderosa trees are the most common pine trees in North America. Their rust-colored trunks can grow to 4 feet wide. They are fire-resistant, which helps the trees survive and grow to great heights. Groups of mature ponderosas grow on either side of the Grand Canyon. Their overlapping branches form "tree islands." These are home to many different types of wildlife.

ARIZONA FESCUE

The shade-loving bunchgrass known as Arizona fescue thrives on the forest floor. Bunchgrasses grow in large clumps. Birds called dark-eyed juncos build their nests under them. They also provide cover for fawns (baby deer) and baby rabbits. Mice, voles, and packrats also eat their seeds.

PYGMY NUTHATCH

Flocks of tiny birds called pygmy nuthatches are common in pine forests. They peep to one another as they look for insects and seeds. A hundred or more may roost together in tree cavities. Year-old males help their parents defend their nests and feed their young.

The Kaibab squirrel is a type of Abert's squirrel. It is only found in the ponderosa pine forests on the canyon's North Rim.

ABERT'S SQUIRREL

Abert's squirrels' only source of food comes from ponderosa pines. They eat the tree's buds, pollen cones, seeds, and the inner bark of twigs. They chase each other around the trunks, build nests in the branches, and dig for fungi, like false truffles, at the roots.

NORTH AMERICAN PORCUPINE

Porcupines are slow-moving but rarely seen. They are large rodents with coats of sharp spines called quills. If startled, they turn their back, stick up their quills and flip their barbed tails. During the day they sleep in dens or treetops. At night they **forage** for plants, twigs, and mineral-rich mud.

MONARCH BUTTERFLY MIGRATIONS

Every fall, millions of monarch butterflies fly south from their breeding grounds in the north. Some pass through the Grand Canyon on their way. They travel thousands of kilometers to spend the winter in the trees of central Mexico or the California coast. These southbound monarchs are known as the "super generation" because they can fly further and live eight times longer than regular monarch butterflies.

BUTTERFLY HIGHWAYS

Monarchs travel on "**flyways**"—routes where wind and good weather help them to fly 25–30 miles a day. In fall, the Colorado River is an important monarch flyway.

THE SUPER GENERATION

When they reach their destination, the super generation monarchs pass the winter clinging to trees. In spring, they mate and the females lay eggs on milkweed plants, then die. Their eggs become a new generation, which flies north to breed. It takes three or four generations to reach the most northerly breeding grounds, as northbound monarchs live only three to eight weeks.

THE MONARCH LIFECYCLE

A monarch egg hatches into a tiny caterpillar. For the first two weeks the caterpillar eats milkweed. It grows 2,000 times larger and sheds its skin five times as it grows.

Then it attaches to a secure spot and hangs upside down. Its skin falls off and uncovers an outer case called a chrysalis. Inside the chrysalis, the caterpillar changes shape.

After one or two weeks, the chrysalis splits open and a butterfly emerges! Once it has emerged, the butterfly pumps fluid into its wings to unfurl them so that it can fly.

SURVIVAL STRATEGIES

Milkweed contains a chemical that makes caterpillars taste bitter. The chemical stays in their bodies so that adult monarchs taste bitter too. Predators learn to avoid them both.

Spider milkweed

Broadleaf milkweed

Horsetail milkweed

PINYON–JUNIPER WOODLAND

Pinyon pines and junipers are small trees about 9 meters tall. They grow together in warm places on the canyon rims and down its rocky walls. Pinyon pines have needles and produce nuts. Junipers have leaves like tiny scales and cones with pulp on the outsides. Many berries and fruits grow on shrubs among the trees providing birds, rodents, and reptiles with lots to eat.

BLACK TARANTULA

Grand Canyon black tarantulas are large and hairy spiders. Pads on their feet feel vibrations from the insects they hunt at night. In the fall, male tarantulas are seen during the daytime looking for females to mate with.

NORTHERN GRASSHOPPER MOUSE

Unlike other mice, northern grasshopper mice are carnivorous—they only eat animals, including other rodents. They kill with a bite, throw back their heads, and then howl into the night in a high-pitched voice.

MOUNTAIN LION

Mountain lions live by themselves in the Grand Canyon's forests. They see very well in the dark. To hunt their prey, like deer or elk, they wait until it is close enough for the lion to leap and sink its teeth into it.

SPOTTED BAT

The Grand Canyon is home to twenty-two species of bat. Spotted bats live in the ponderosa forest in summer and **migrate** down to the warmer places in winter. Bats use **echolocation** to find their prey at night—they send out squeaks that bounce off the moths they hunt and travel back to their big ears.

RAPTORS

If you've visited the Grand Canyon, chances are you might have seen a **raptor** soaring high up in the sky. Raptors are birds like hawks, eagles, falcons, owls, and vultures. Thirty species of these raptors hunt in the park. When their keen eyes spot prey from a distance, they dive from the sky and grab it with eight sharp claws called talons.

PEREGRINE FALCON

Peregrine falcons dive up to 185 miles per hour to stun their prey. They hunt mostly birds and bats.

ZONE-TAILED HAWK

Zone-tailed hawks soar in circles on drafts of rising warm air called thermals. Once they spot their prey, they drop them from low heights. They nest at Grand Canyon in summer and migrate south in autumn.

CALIFORNIA CONDOR

The California condor is North America's largest land bird, with a wingspan of 9.5 feet! By the 1900s, condors were almost extinct in the wild. In 1987, scientists stepped in and captured the last twenty-seven wild condors. Safe in pens, their numbers grew until they could be released into the wild again. Today, there are more than 300 condors in the wild, with one hundred living around the Grand Canyon.

MEXICAN SPOTTED OWL

These large owls live in the canyon's caves, where they are safe from peregrine falcons. People once thought the owls only lived in forests until scientists looking for California condors accidentally discovered Mexican spotted owls in the canyon's large, open caves.

DESERT SCRUB

It is very hot and dry in the desert scrub, so plants that grow here must be able to survive with little water. Only shrubs and smaller plants grow here, as it is too dry for trees. During the spring, insects visit flowers and many birds arrive to eat the insects. It gets very hot in the summer months, so animals like birds depart to cooler locations. These warmer summer months are perfect for reptiles though, which is why eighteen species of lizards and twenty-two species of snakes can be found here.

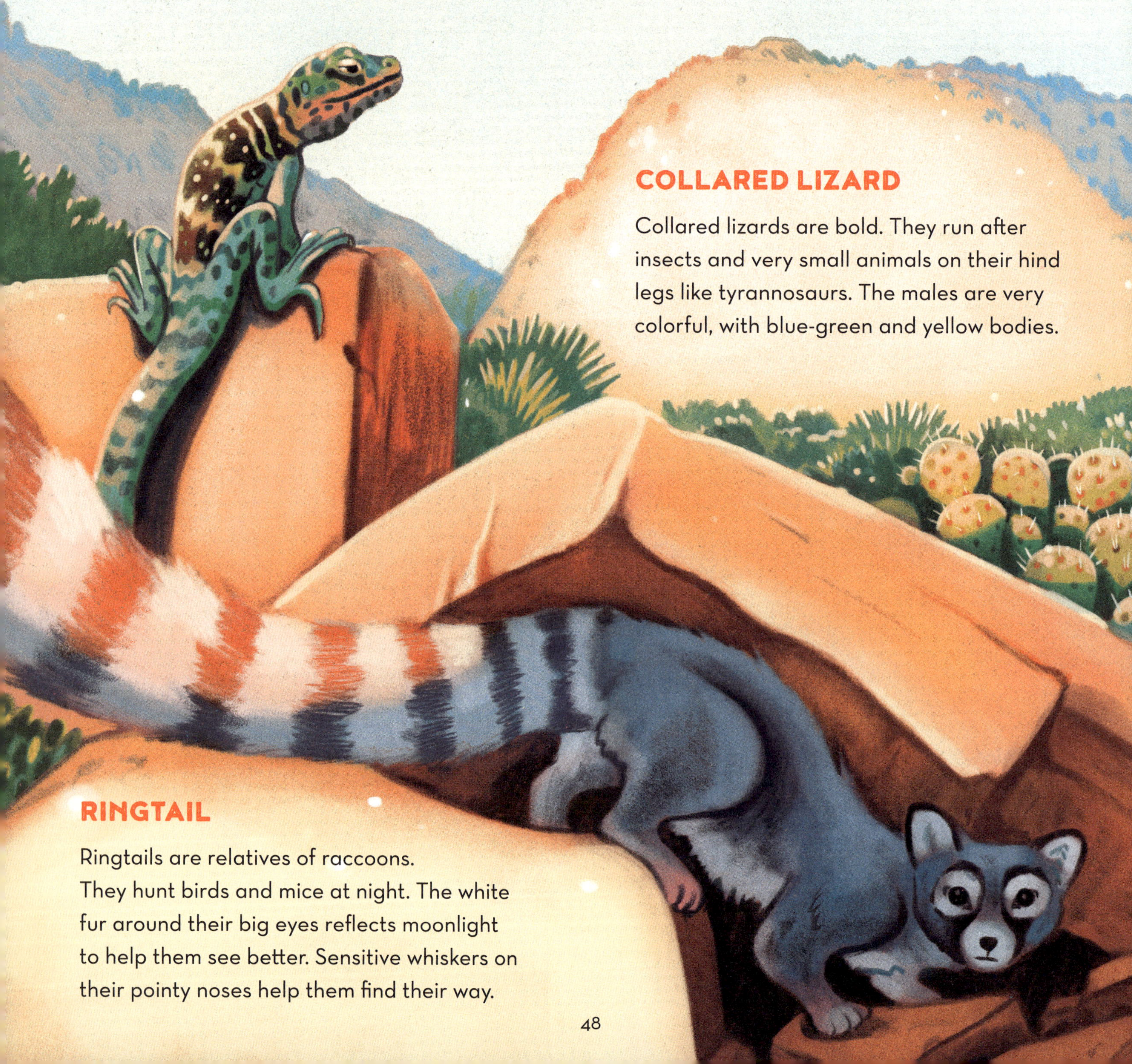

COLLARED LIZARD

Collared lizards are bold. They run after insects and very small animals on their hind legs like tyrannosaurs. The males are very colorful, with blue-green and yellow bodies.

RINGTAIL

Ringtails are relatives of raccoons. They hunt birds and mice at night. The white fur around their big eyes reflects moonlight to help them see better. Sensitive whiskers on their pointy noses help them find their way.

DESERT BIGHORN SHEEP

Desert bighorn sheep live in steep and rocky places where predators can't catch them. Males rear up, run at each other, and knock their horns together to show who's boss.

JAVELINA

Javelinas woof and grunt as they travel in groups, called "squadrons," of a dozen or more. They have very tough mouths and can eat almost anything. Their favorite food is prickly pear cactus.

CACTI

Cacti are fleshy plants that grow in hot, dry places with little water. Their green stems full of slimy pulp and waxy skin keep them from drying out. Cactus roots spread just under the ground to soak in rain the minute it falls. Cacti have sharp spines to save water and discourage predators. Some cacti look like strings of sausages or flat pads. Others look like barrels. They have sweet, juicy berries.

CACTUS BEE

Cactus bees live alone and make nests in the ground. They drink nectar from many plants but collect pollen to feed their young only from cactus flowers.

CLARETCUP HEDGEHOG CACTUS

Claretcup hedgehog cacti have bright red flowers and small red fruit. They can form mounds of 500 stems packed together.

GRIZZLYBEAR PRICKLY PEAR CACTUS

Grizzlybear prickly pear cacti have dense spines 1 to 7 inches long. Their round pads can form clumps up to 10 feet across.

CACTUS WREN

These small birds can be spotted perched on the tops of cacti, ready to chase away predators. Most of the water they need comes from cactus fruit. They often make their nests in the safety of prickly cactus branches. Their nests are the size and shape of a football.

TEDDYBEAR CHOLLA

Teddybear cholla have edible buds and green flowers. Their long yellow spines with sharp hooks make them look fuzzy. Cholla joints come off and root to make more plants. Woodrats camouflage and protect their nests with them.

REPTILES

The Grand Canyon is home to many types of reptiles including snakes, lizards, and the elusive desert tortoise. Reptiles are cold-blooded, so they need sunshine to stay warm. Their bodies are covered in scales to hold in water instead of fur to keep them warm. Reptiles usually eat insects, mice, and other reptiles. Most lay eggs and do not raise their young. There are forty-one species of reptiles in the park.

GRAND CANYON RATTLESNAKE

The Grand Canyon rattlesnake eats once every few weeks. Pits above its nose sense heat from rodents, birds, and lizards. Its fangs inject a poison before they swallow their prey whole.

The Grand Canyon rattlesnake is only found around the Grand Canyon.

GREATER SHORT-HORNED LIZARD

Greater short-horned lizards don't need to flee from predators—they have a few tricks to frighten them away. They squirt blood from their eyes and suck in air to double their size.

SONORAN MOUNTAIN KINGSNAKE

These snakes may bite but they are not poisonous. They hide under rocks and slither out to strangle mice or small snakes. They hibernate underground or among rocks in winter.

CHUCKWALLA

These large, flat-bodied lizards eat leaves, buds, flowers, and fruit. Chuckwallas protect themselves from predators by crawling between rocks and inflating their wrinkly bodies until they are safely wedged in tight.

LIFE ALONG THE WATER'S EDGE

Riparian areas have the greatest density and diversity of wildlife in the park. Seeps and springs create oases for insects and amphibians along cracks in the canyon walls and between different layers of rocks. Hanging gardens of ferns and rare snails attract birds to dripping water.

Coyote willow, alder, and cottonwood trees shade springs and creeks flowing down smaller side-canyons to the river.

THIRST QUENCHING

Amphibians like red-spotted toads, tiger salamanders, and canyon tree frogs live in riparian areas. Mammals such as coyotes, ringtails, spotted skunks, and bats visit them for water and to hunt.

BURSTING WITH BIRDS

Forty-eight bird species nest along the banks of the Colorado River, including great blue herons and the endangered southwestern willow flycatcher. Some birds fly up to eighteen miles twice a day to reach these areas.

Belted kingfishers dig tunnels up to 6 feet deep for their nests.

Beavers are North America's largest rodents. They eat cottonwood leaves and bark that they hold with their nimble front paws.

PLENTY TO EAT

Songbirds called American dippers live along these creeks year-round, using their wings to swim underwater and hunt insect larvae and a small fish called speckled dace.

CHANGING ENVIRONMENTS

Every plant and animal in an ecosystem is important. The ecosystem suffers when an animal becomes extinct or is removed from the landscape. But it can also suffer when a new animal arrives. Some of the animals we see at Grand Canyon today were not there one hundred years ago. Some were brought in by people, others came by themselves as habitats changed due to climate change.

BACK FROM THE BRINK

For a long time California condors were extinct in the wild. Scientists knew they once lived around the Grand Canyon after discovering an 11,000-year-old condor skull. Condors eat dead animals and keep the ecosystem healthy. They were reintroduced to the Grand Canyon in 1992. It's good to have them back!

KEEP YOUR DISTANCE

Elk are not native to the Grand Canyon. Wildlife rangers brought them to the area for hunting in the early 1900s. Now around one hundred elk live in the forests on the South Rim. Elk are not adapted to the dry climate and their search for water often brings them close to people. They can weigh 700 pounds and have long, sharp antlers, which makes them very dangerous. Elk also destroy some plants by eating them down to the ground.

TRAMPLING HOOVES

One hundred years ago, a ranch owner brought a herd of bison to his land near the Grand Canyon. He planned to breed them with his cattle to create animals that produce more meat. His idea failed and the bison moved up onto the North Rim. They pollute the streams and trample the plants.

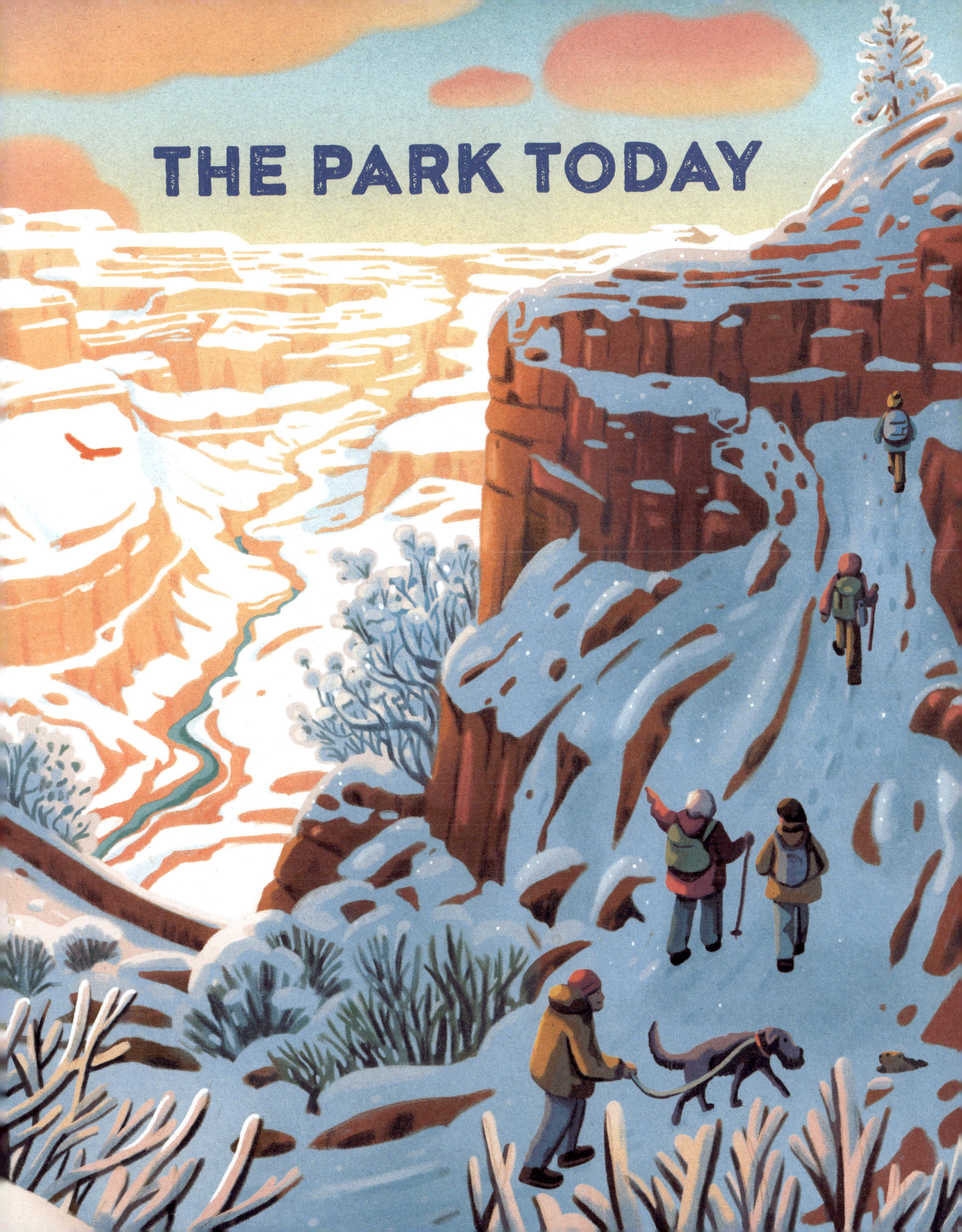
THE PARK TODAY

DARK SKIES

Patterns of bright stars and planets called **constellations** fill the night sky over the Grand Canyon. From early times, people have watched how the movements of stars and planets mark events in the natural world. Constellations have inspired art, thinking, religion, and science for thousands of years.

ORION THE HUNTER

The constellation Orion is easiest to see from the Grand Canyon in winter. It is named after a hunter in Greek mythology. Orion appears to be facing a constellation called Taurus, the bull, as it charges toward him. Orion's Belt is a made up of three very bright stars in a straight line that make it easy to find the rest of the constellation.

HARMFUL LIGHT

Once upon a time, anyone could see vivid stars at night no matter where they lived. Now the glow of streetlights and buildings in towns and cities hides the stars from many of us. This is known as "light pollution." It is harmful to wildlife that hunt and feed under cover of darkness and harmful to the environment too, as it wastes energy.

DARK SKY PARK

Grand Canyon National Park is an International Dark Sky Park, which makes it perfect for stargazing. It is far from the lights of any city and restrictions on the use of artificial light within the park mean that its clear, dark skies are protected for the future.

GUIDED BY THE STARS

Elders of the Kaibab Paiute Tribe would wake up early, face the horizon to the east, and look for signs from the stars and constellations that would indicate it was time to plant or time to harvest.

THE MILKY WAY

The Milky Way is a spinning disk of stars called a spiral galaxy. One of those stars is our sun. From the Grand Canyon, the best time to see the Milky Way is from May through October. It looks like a stream of clouds and stars pouring through the night. When there is no moon, the Milky Way can be so bright that we cast a shadow on the ground when we stand in its light.

As the Earth spins around the sun, we see different parts of the sky. Constellations appear in the east and move to the west as the year goes by. There are eighty-eight major constellations.

URSA MAJOR

Different cultures have different names for the same constellations. *Ursa Major*, a Latin name that means "the larger bear," is the third-largest constellation. It can be seen from the Grand Canyon throughout the year. Its seven brightest stars—at the rear end and tail of the bear—are known as the Big Dipper, or The Plough. Two of its stars point to a third star named Polaris, which is also called the North Star. As the Earth spins on its axis, Polaris appears in the same place above the north pole. Since earliest times, people have used Polaris to find their way at night.

PEOPLE OF THE PARK

At least 5 million people visit Grand Canyon National Park every year. During the busiest months, they are welcomed by close to 400 National Park Service staff, hundreds of volunteers, and the many who work for hotels, restaurants, and shops.

Rangers: *Rangers lead nature walks and give campground talks at night. They hike backcountry trails and raft down the Colorado River to lend help where needed and enforce park rules.*

Park scientists: *Park scientists hike, helicopter, or raft to study springs, caves, wildlife, and plants. They collect information to help guide decisions about taking care of the park.*

Archaeologists: *Archaeologists work with volunteers, museums, and universities to uncover and protect the traces of long-ago people. They also work with tribes to understand their ancient dwellings and artwork.*

Wildland crews: *When conditions are just right, wildland crews carefully set controlled forest fires to allow new plants to flourish and prevent destructive wildfires. If a dangerous fire starts, they work around the clock to put it out.*

Crews: *Crews keep trails open by removing rockfalls, building low walls along steep drops, and filling in holes caused by rainstorms. They maintain old buildings and plow snow off the roads.*

Volunteers: *Volunteers help with almost every activity in the park. High school and college students give talks and assist park scientists during the summer. Teams of young Native American people work to protect native plant life and monitor archaeological sites. Volunteers also advise hikers, answer questions at visitor centers, and help with the museum study collection.*

Astronomers: *Astronomers set up telescopes to help visitors find their way among the stars and learn about the values of dark night skies.*

PROTECTING PLANTS

Native plants are plants that have evolved naturally within an ecosystem over thousands of years. An ecosystem's animals will often depend on native species for survival. Sometimes humans introduce non-native plants that can damage fragile ecosystems.

SAVING SEEDS

Crews of park botanists and volunteers collect seeds to grow thousands of plants for restoring or expanding Grand Canyon National Park's native plant communities. They will even rescue native plants from trampling or construction and replant them safely nearby.

Crews transplanted the endangered sentry milk-vetch and the rare Tusayan fameflower from areas where they were threatened to safer habitats.

REMOVE AND RESTORE

Park botanists and volunteers also work together to remove non-native plants from the park. Large numbers of non-native tamarisk trees had spread along the Colorado River in the park. Tamarisk trees prevent native trees, like willows, from growing so crews have removed hundreds of them from the park to protect and restore native plant communities there.

POLLINATOR GARDENS

Park botanists and volunteers have also planted pollinator gardens on both sides of the canyon. To plant the gardens, the team collected seeds from over sixty native species of plant. The gardens grow native milkweeds for monarch butterfly caterpillars and nectar-rich flowering plants for all kinds of pollinators.

CHANGING CLIMATE

Due to climate change, the canyon's habitats are changing and slowly drying out. Although the average amount of rain and snow is not much lower than in the past, higher temperatures are speeding up the evaporation of wetlands, seeps, and springs, all vital sources of water for much of the park's wildlife.

RISING TEMPERATURES

As temperatures increase, plants of the canyon's life zones are beginning to grow higher up the canyon walls. The animals that rely on these plants follow in search of food. Bighorn sheep have started to travel down to the river for water because springs that are higher up are dry. Whereas up on the rim, forest fires are more likely to happen.

LIMITING HUMAN USE

With water becoming more scarce, Grand Canyon National Park is working hard to limit the human use of water and is improving the water distribution system to prevent waste. The US Congress is debating laws to outlaw mining in the Grand Canyon area, which contaminates and uses up the aquifer.

WATER LEVELS

The Colorado River carries much less water now than it did only a few decades ago. The river's native fish struggle to survive because Glen Canyon Dam changed their habitat so much. Park scientists are working with the dam's managers to release enough water for the fish to spawn in spring and thrive at other stages of their life cycle too.

A PLACE TO INSPIRE

Grand Canyon National Park reminds us of what an amazing planet we live on. It shows us how mountains and canyons form, and how rivers can shape the land. Every creature we watch brings us closer to the natural world. A forest of huge ponderosas inspires us to respect and care for nature. Knowing that people who lived here long ago thrived with what they found around them helps us consider what we humans truly need and what we don't. The canyon challenges us to be our best.

The Grand Canyon also teaches us about time. Cascading stars shimmering in its dark skies reveals the splendor of the universe. We understand that change will come but life will adapt and flourish.

GLOSSARY

Amphibians: Cold-blooded animals that live on land and in water

Ancestor: A person who lived in the past and was in the same family as someone alive now

Archaeologist: A scientist who studies human history and culture by digging up artifacts

Artifact: An object made by humans that is studied by archaeologists and gives us information about the past

Botanist: A scientist who studies plants

Brachiopods: Marine animals with shells and a pair of tentacles

Ceremony: A type of formal event

Clubmosses: A group of ancient land plants

Crinoids: A group of marine invertebrates

Constellation: A group of stars in the night sky

Echolocation: A process used by some animals to locate objects using sound waves

Ecosystem: All the living and non-living things in an area, including plants and animals

Expedition: A journey made in order to do something

Flyway: A route that birds or insects travel along

Forage: To go from place to place searching for things to eat

Fossil: The remains of plants or animals that lived a long time ago

Geologist: A scientist that studies the surface of Earth and what it is made of

Kiva: A Pueblo Indian ceremonial structure that is usually round and partly underground

Mantle: The mostly solid bulk of Earth's interior

Megafauna: Large land animals of the last ice age such as mammoths

Metamorphic: A rock formed from pre-existing rock that has changed through heat and pressure

Migration: When animals move from one place to another on a regular basis usually to find food or warmer weather

Native: A plant or creature that is found in a certain ecosystem and has not been introduced to the area by humans

Paleozoic era: 541–252 million years ago

Pueblos: A settlement that has houses made of stone, adobe, and wood

Pithouse: A house built in the ground and used for shelter

Plankton: Drifting organisms that live in the surface layers of the ocean

Plateau: Raised, flat-surfaced areas with cliffs or steep slopes on one or more sides

Raptor: A large bird that hunts or kills other animals

Reptile: A cold-blooded animal that lays eggs and has scales on its body

Reservation: Land set aside for a special use

Seedferns: A group of plants that is now extinct

Tectonic plates: Broken pieces of Earth's crust

Trilobites: Prehistoric animals related to today's insects, woodlice, and crabs

Vertebrate: An animal that has a backbone inside their body

INDEX

WRITTEN BY SUSAN LAMB

Susan Lamb has authored thirty books and numerous articles and essays exploring the relationships between the natural world and the human spirit, especially in the traditional cultures of the American Southwest and Europe. Born in California, she moved often, residing briefly in Kodiak, Alaska, and Wiesbaden, Germany, as well in several towns and cities in California. She served with the National Park Service for seven years, the last four as Desert View District Ranger at Grand Canyon National Park, and led study tours to natural areas in the American West for the Smithsonian National Associates Program and other clients. She lives outside Flagstaff, Arizona, with her husband, photographer Tom Bean.

ILLUSTRATED BY SEAN LEWIS

Sean Lewis was born in Toronto (Tkaronto), the ancestral and traditional territory of the Mississaugas of the Credit, the Haudenosaune, the Anishnabe and the Huron-Wendat. He received a Bachelor of Design from OCADU in 2011 and has worked as a concept artist/matte painter for film/television, a sessional university instructor, and a freelance illustrator. In 2021 he illustrated and art directed the Annie Award nominated music video "Featherweight" for Fleet Foxes. His first picture book, *I'll Get to the Bottom of This!* was written by Daniel Kwan (writer and director of *Everything Everywhere All At Once*) and published by A24 in 2022.

WITH EXPERT HELP FROM

Lance Polingyouma

A member of the Hopi Tribe of Arizona, Lance grew up as a farmer and cowboy, raising all kinds of animals and plants and exploring the desert he calls home. Lance went to high school and college in Massachusetts, where he studied anthropology. He currently lives on the Hopi Reservation, where he is an elementary school instructor.

ALSO IN THE SERIES

EVEREST

By Sangma Francis and Lisk Feng

There is a place where a mountain grows. It is the highest spot on Earth, the ultimate challenge for mountain-climbing adventurers, the towering figure of Sagarmatha, the Goddess of the Sky.

Welcome to Mount Everest.

THE GREAT BARRIER REEF

By Sangma Francis and Lisk Feng

In the waters where Australia meets the vast Pacific Ocean, grows the world's most famous reef. Schools of fish dart among the colorful corals, octopuses hide in dark corners, and sharks patrol the clear waters above.

Welcome to the Great Barrier Reef.

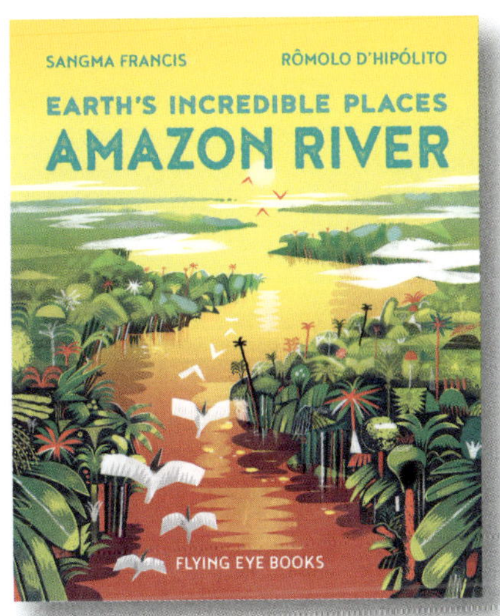

AMAZON RIVER

By Sangma Francis and Rômolo D'Hipólito

Beginning with a tiny trickle high in the mountains, smaller streams join until they form the world's largest river. Crossing a continent, it winds through lush rain forests until it meets the ocean. From piranhas to the giant anaconda, this mighty waterway is home to the world's most incredible ecosystem.

Welcome to the Amazon River.

YELLOWSTONE

By Catherine Ard and Bianca Austria

In the Rocky Mountains of America there is a place where eagles soar over jagged peaks, waterfalls plunge down rocky cliffs, and icy forests ring with the howls of wolves. Where mud bubbles, springs steam, and water explodes from deep underground.

Welcome to Yellowstone.